Helping Someone Through Grief by Cara Brzezicki.

Published by Jazzie Beans Publishing.

www.JazzieBeans.com

No part of this publication may be reproduced in whole or in part, or stored in a retrieval system, or transmitted in any form or by any means, electronic mechanical, photocopying, recording, or otherwise, without written permission of the Publisher/Author. For information regarding permission, write to welcome@JazzieBeans.com.

ISBN-13: 9781733831765

Text & Illustration Copyright ©2022 by Cara Brzezicki
Illustrations by Kasie Lien

DEDICATION

To Brooke and the fabulous nurses on the labor and delivery floor at UC Health in Highlands Ranch, CO for helping me through the loss of my stillborn daughter. Also, to my beautiful daughter, Corynn Jae, who I will hold again in heaven some day.

ACKNOWLEDGMENTS

I would like to thank my husband and two boys for always supporting me and being there for me. My husband is going through this as well and I cannot imagine my life without him.

I would like to thank my parents and my friends and family for being there for me during this awful season. I am so blessed to have you all in my life!

I want to thank Jamie Stewart and Walk With Me nonprofit for all of the comfort, support and lovely gifts that helped my boys, my husband and myself.

Without my faith in God, I could not have written this book and I would not be where I am today. My church, Red Rocks Church, has the most amazing pastors and people and have helped my family and I on our healing journey~thank you!

Helping Someone Through Grief

A quick guide for adults

Written by
Cara Brzezicki

Illustrations by
Kasie Lien

Dear, dear reader (who has suffered a loss),

May I just say that I am so saddened and hurt for your broken heart. I am so sorry for your loss. I know those words will be heard the most and you may become annoyed, hurt, numb, appreciative, and a variety of other emotions. Honestly though, I truly am sorry and wish I could hug you or hold you to tell you that what you are going through is so hard and I am so saddened for you.

People mean well and their hearts hurt for you, but nothing compared to the hurt you are experiencing. Your pain is real and you should never have to minimize your pain. When you receive unsolicited advice (because you will and like I said, people mean well, but they are not equipped to handle a grieving person), you can let them know how you feel and if you do not want to let them know, you can just ignore them. They will use "at least" statements, which are not helpful and not empathetic statements, but sympathetic statements.

Try to avoid those who are not supportive of your grieving process. It is okay! You will have happy moments too, and that is okay. Feel all the feels and every feeling is okay (except if you feel like harming yourself. Then, please contact 911, your best friend, your spouse, anyone you feel comfortable talking to, or even me at Welcome@JazzieBeans.com. Put in the email subject line: URGENT and I will contact you right away!!)

There are resources in the back of this book that may help you. Please give this book or recommend this book to those you want to help you. I wrote it for those who want to help you, but do not know how to, or people who think they know how to help, but really do not.

Remember, you are loved, you are special, and what you are going through is awful! Please feel all of the feels and please reach out if you need advice or help. I ♥ you!!

Dear reader (the one who wants to help someone who has suffered a loss), Thank you so much for caring for your grieving friend, relative, spouse, your special someone. You are an amazing asset to them! This book is meant to help you be a great listening ear to help your grieving someone. We all mean well to help those that are grieving, but we truly are not equipped with the knowledge to help properly.

You are already a great person for wanting to help and help in the best way. Thank you from the bottom of my heart for caring.

I created this book as a quick guide to help you help your friend, relative, etc. I know that time is precious and reading a huge book takes a lot of time. My hope is that this book is a quick read so you can help your grieving person right away!

Let's start with the difference between sympathy and empathy. According to the dictionary: sympathy is feelings of pity and sorrow for someone else's misfortunes. Empathy is the ability to understand and share the feelings of another.

The real difference is seeing the sadness (sympathy) and feeling the sadness (empathy).

Sympathy

Empathy

Now, I do not want you to constantly be sad for your grieving person, but to tap into a bit of that feeling will help you be a good listening ear.

According to Dr. Brené Brown, "Empathy fuels connection. Sympathy drives disconnection." (In the back of this book is a list of resources, and one of them is a YouTube video discussing empathy vs. sympathy. It is great for any age.)

Here are some steps to help you show empathy:

- Be an active listener

    ~ actually listen to what your grieving person is saying. This is not the time to share your insight or words of wisdom. Unsolicited advice really makes the person feel worse!!

- Try to understand their emotions and where they are coming from. Put yourself in their shoes.

    (I know you have heard this a million times, but it really does help ☺).

- Do not judge! This is usually hard for most people. Not because we are trying to be harsh or mean, it is just because we are human.

~ giving your grieving someone room to vent or talk without judgement will be so helpful. We all have to get it out with someone. If that someone is you, then you truly are a beautiful light. Shine brightly and use this book to your advantage.

~ when someone is grieving, they have around 15 emotions going at once or cyclically or a few at a time. There is an array of emotions and they can be so confusing to them and to you.

~ here are the typical emotions for grief:

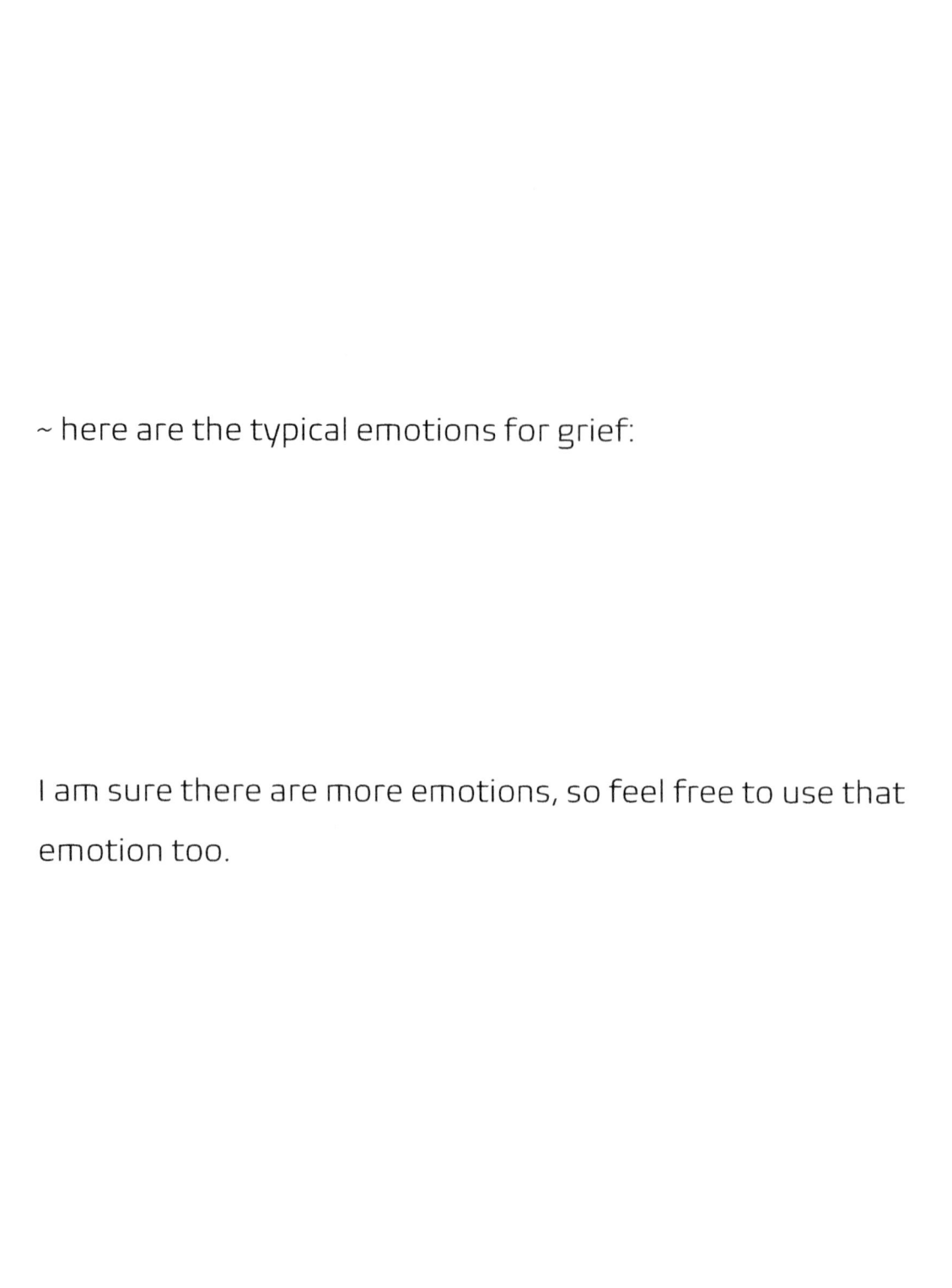

I am sure there are more emotions, so feel free to use that emotion too.

Sadness Guilt Joy Gratitude

Anger Anxiety Confusion

Frustration

Yearning Fear

Envy

Numbness

Hope Relief

Resentment

Whatever that person is feeling is okay (I say this a few times throughout the book 😊). While you are actively listening to your grieving someone and putting yourself in their shoes, you can ask them if they just want you to listen to them, like being a sound board. If they do want you to speak, remember to not use "at least" statements or judgement statements.

Relaying how they are feeling and telling them that it is okay to feel that way is perfect. Continue to say, "I am sorry," and it is perfectly okay to say, "I do not even know what to say." Honestly, your grieving person just wants to be heard.

Also, using statements like, "I am here for you", "I do not have the right words to say", "I love you so much", "You are so loved!", "I am sending you prayers (or love or hugs or all three, whatever you feel comfortable saying here)", will be so helpful.

Please remember to not finish their sentences. You are an active listener! Remember active listener 😊.

I truly hope that this book has helped you to help your grieving person. As a mom who recently lost her daughter, I received so much love and condolences. I also received so much unsolicited advice and "at least" statements. They were super hurtful, but I knew that the people saying these things meant it with kindness.

They just were not educated in the grieving process. That is why I wrote this short book. I want to give this out to those who are trying to help but are lost for words. I do not want your grieving person to receive the words that I received.

People just want to help and most of the time they do not know how to. But you, my friend, are better equipped now.

RESOURCES

- ✓ www.stillstandingmag.com
  (child loss & fertility)
- ✓ www.everystep.org
  (guide for children's loss)
- ✓ www.freespirit.com
  (loss of a friend)
- ✓ www.sands.org.uk
  (loss of a grandbaby)
- ✓ www.frienshiphospital.com
  (loss of a pet)
- ✓ https://youtu.be/1Evwgu369Jw
  (Brene Brown YouTube video)

If you have time and liked this book, do you mind reviewing it on Amazon please?

https://amazon.com/dp/1733831762

I appreciate you and 🩶 you so much!

You are Awesome!

Thank you so much,
I truly appreciate it!

CARA

Other books by this author

Jazzie Beans Series

Printed in Great Britain
by Amazon